The Millionaire Booklet How to Get Super Rich

Grant Cardone

The Millionaire Booklet:
How to Get Super Rich

ISBN 978-0-9903554-5-8

To order more copies for you or your team, go to MillionaireBooklet.com or contact Grant Cardone Enterprises at 310-777-0255.

First Edition

Table of Contents

Preface

I was inspired to write this book after attending a charity event. It was a Sunday night when a couple of hundred people showed up for dinner knowing they were going to be asked to give money. The target was two million dollars. As I looked around to see who could actually pay, I thought the target impossible. The room was filled with hardworking, super generous people who had already given much of their money, even borrowed money, and many were volunteering their time. Some had done all three.

I could tell they all wanted to do more, but they were just tapped out. About twenty percent of the total was raised by fifty people. There was another $500,000 raised by four families, still leaving us one million dollars short.

The last million was donated by one guy and, the audience was thrilled and amazed. People were crying, and proud we had achieved this vital goal of funding this worthy project. As I looked around, watching everyone celebrate, I realized there was not a person in the room who didn't want to be the guy who gave the last million.

I came home that night, inspired, and told my wife, "I'm going to write a book to teach people how to become millionaires," and that night I wrote this book. The Millionaire Booklet was written without a ghostwriter, impressive words, or a bunch of economic facts. In fact, it was written in two hours.

Forgive me in advance for its simplicity. I hope to make

millionaires with this small booklet—not award-winning writers or economists. I am not trying to impress you with what I have accomplished in my life or how much I know. The reality is, what I have created financially in my life is very simple, and that is why it will work for you.

I want to help you reach millionaire status, even get rich, if you believe that you deserve to be the person in the room that writes the check for a million dollars, ten million or even 100 million—let's roll.

GC

Introduction

In The Millionaire Booklet: How to Become Super Rich, I want to simplify the process of becoming a millionaire and, if you want, even super rich. This isn't some pie in the sky, out of reach big claim. I know it is attainable because I have used the information here and done it. I know with 100 percent certainty that anyone can do this and even more if they do the work. Regardless of your current economic condition, where you live, or what you do you can become wealthy. I also believe it's your responsibility to do so.

In case you don't know anything about my story, I'll reveal that when I was young I made a commitment to creating wealth for myself. Since then I have worked very hard and created generational wealth that is probably indestructible. I say "probably" because I am not naïve enough to underestimate the levels of economic manipulation and insanity present on this planet.

While I made my commitment to get rich at sixteen, I was still broke at twenty-five. Then I started studying the wealthy, using the principles of wealth creation and codifying what worked and didn't. It has been a long haul for me. I remember saving my first $10,000— then one day realizing it was $100,000. By the time I was in my early thirties, I had my first million set aside. Since then, I have built five companies that produce over $100 million a year in sales, created a net worth well over $100 million and own an income-producing real estate portfolio worth over $400 million.

You may be saying, "Good for you, Mr. Cardone, but can you actually show other people how to do what you do?" While I can't guarantee you will have the kind of results I have there are others duplicating the financial success I have created by employing these principles. Here are a few of them:

- Dale C. was fifty-four years of age and had fifty-six dollars to his name when he created over $10 million in net worth and a dependable monthly income using the eight simple steps included here.

- Jarrod G. was twenty-eight when he started following the eight simple steps; in four years was a millionaire with three dependable flows of income.

- David F. went from making $8,000 a month to $50,000 a month.

- DJay H. was making $38,000 annually in sales and increased to $135,000 annually.

- Robert F. followed this information and went from $18,000/year to $360,000/year in 24 months.

- Diane C. was sixty-five when she employed these millionaire strategies and made more money in the following year than she had made in her entire lifetime.

Chapter 1

Getting Rich Is Not a Fantasy

How to become a millionaire or multi-millionaire or even hecta-millionaire (100 million units) isn't taught in schools or colleges. In fact, most of society frowns on anyone who talks about getting rich; some even protest against those who have created financial independence.

It's a funny thing that schools teach you how to read and write, how to do math, how to know history and geography, and how to pass a test—but they never broach the subject of how to get rich. Getting super rich seems to be a topic reserved for fantasies, movies, and drunken what-if games. Most have come to believe that becoming a millionaire is for the lucky sperm club, business owners, gold diggers, lottery winners, athletes, rappers, and inventors. But it's not true. Millionaires and the super rich come from all walks of life. In fact, just to debunk one of the myths, I'll tell you that four out of five millionaires today work for someone else.

The reason most people never get rich is that they never even consider it a possibility. They are convinced by those close to them to simply be satisfied with whatever their financial situation is. The other reason is that people fundamentally do not understand money. Very few people know how to get money, even fewer know how to keep it, and almost no one knows how to multiply it. Just look around and you will see signs of this everywhere.

Even in one of the richest countries in the world, America, 76 percent of people live paycheck to paycheck, some 50 percent of Americans have no money for retirement, and 47 percent of Americans don't have

$400 for an emergency. If these statistics were true in a poor country, it would be one thing, but America is considered a wealthy country.

"Very few people even know how to get money, even fewer know how to keep it, and almost no one knows how to multiply it."

Turn on the television or go online and you will see endless, ridiculous financial advice. Financial pundits suggest saving tricks where your path to wealth is finding the lowest price for a product or putting more air in your tires to save gas. This piece of advice always cracks me up: "If you don't drink coffee out, you'll save another $700 a year." You can save $700 a year for the next fifty years and you won't be rich, you'll just be old.

Another pundit preaches all debt is bad, and that by avoiding debt you will somehow be financially free. "Never borrow money under any circumstance," the previously bankrupt advisor promotes. He overlooks the reality that almost all the super rich have used debt to multiply their wealth.

Flip the channel and you'll see fancy graphics making a case that you should turn your money over to the boys on Wall Street who, smarter than you, will invest in stocks, bonds, and financial instruments they can't even explain. Ask your parents for money advice and they will recite their path: get a good job, buy a house, contribute to your 401k, be grateful you have more than most, and pray everything goes right.

I have never wanted to just have "enough," in fact, truth be known, I have always wanted to be rich. While I do believe in prayer, I don't expect God to take care of my finances and I certainly don't want to leave it up to everything "going right." At a very young age, I noticed how the people who made the decisions and had the power of choice all seemed to be the people with money. I wanted to be one of them. I didn't want money for the sake of money, but to be able to have the power of choice.

At the age of eight, one of my first experiences with money was walking to the local grocery store. I had a quarter in my pocket to spend at the store. I was excited, giddy, and I felt powerful. I was walking to the store with my brother fondling my quarter when I dropped it in the street and it rolled into a manhole. I got onto my hands and knees, only to discover my arms were too short to retrieve the quarter. I got up wet, dirty, angry, and wanting to cry.

I remember going home and telling my father how I had lost my quarter. My father said to me, "You shouldn't play with money." My grandfather later grabbed me and said, "Son, the problem isn't simply that you lost the quarter; the problem is that it was your only quarter." Since that loss I have been fascinated with the idea of amassing enough money so no single event or loss would ever cause me to be without.

Chapter 2

Where You Get Your Advice

Word of warning: for this to work you need to start being very selective about where you get your advice. Tell someone you are reading a book about how to get super rich and they will most likely tell you it's impossible. Just try it right now, call a few friends and I assure you at least one of them will say, "Really? The only person who is going to get rich is the guy who wrote the book."

You see, part of the problem is that most get financial advice from people who are struggling with or who have given up on money. Most of the advice we get about money is from people close to us who either don't have money or have given up on it. Some of the people you get advice from have never even thought financial freedom possible.

You must look beyond the dumb advice of family, television pundits, blogs, get-rich articles, cute quotes on Instagram, and silly little sayings.

Look beyond all the noise and confusion about money and you will discover a select group of people who have created enormous wealth. I am talking about the top percentile of the wealthiest people on planet earth. Like magnets of wealth and prosperity, they appear to magically prosper no matter what happens, some doing better in bad times than good times.

These are the people you should study and model your financial journey on. Be very selective where you get your financial advice and never take advice from a quitter or a pretender. There are many pretenders out there and even more who have simply quit on financial freedom.

I tell you this because where I got my advice early on was mostly from observing my surroundings. I organically learned from my immediate environment and adopted the philosophies of those closest to me. I grew up in the middle class. My father worked very hard to create a middle class life for us and this was a big accomplishment for them. Both my mother and father were both brought up poor. My dad made it into the middle class, and shortly afterward he died at the young age of fifty-two.

"Never take advice from a quitter or a pretender."

My mother had no knowledge of money and was left with the responsibility to raise five kids on just a little bit of money from my father's life insurance. My mom was scared, even overwhelmed. Every day she was playing defense trying to figure out how to make ends meet. I felt powerless. I couldn't help her, or so I thought.

My mother's mantras were, "Waste nothing," "Turn off the lights," "Only use what you need," "Save everything," and "Be grateful." By the time I was sixteen, I was fed up watching my mother in a never-ending state of fear. One day I told her, "I am going to get rich someday so I don't have to worry about money. When I do, I am going to help a lot of people." My mother thought I was being an ungrateful brat, but I wasn't. I wasn't grateful because I hated how our life was and as a result I have spent the past forty years trying to change that for myself and others.

Getting rich is a taboo topic in our society. Go outside and tell someone, "I am going to become super rich," and they will think you are crazy. Get rich and then openly tell people, "I am rich," and society will label you a greedy, gluttonous, elitist pig. Tell them you are poor and they will show you sympathy, but tell them you are rich and they will despise you.

The truth is, getting rich—even super rich—shouldn't be taboo, it should be your battle cry. Last year I helped raise more than $100 million for charities. I remember a time when I couldn't lend you a dollar, I was so broke.

Getting rich is not only possible, it is vital to your survival and your ability to help those you love. We live on an economic planet. Every day, every one of us is confronted with money requirements and limitations: from shopping at the grocery store, to feeding yourself, to taking care of your kids and parents, to funding yourself through old age, to taking care of unexpected setbacks.

> *"Getting rich—even super rich—shouldn't be taboo, it should be your battle cry."*

The entire subject of money is greatly misunderstood. What is money? Where did it come from? Who decides what it's worth? What is enough? How do I invest it? When do I have enough to invest? Hell, most people don't even know what they pay in taxes. Most people have more money saved when they are under the age of ten than when they get out of college. It's crazy, when you think about it. How can a kid who knows nothing about money have more money than an adult with a degree?

The reality is, most of us have incorrect knowledge about money from our upbringing. When you are brought up poor or middle class, you inherit the beliefs of the poor and the middle class. You're stuck with their ideas. The simplicity of money and economics is not nearly as complicated as the schools, universities, economists, and financial channels make it out to be. Money, economics, and amassing financial freedom is actually very simple.

For instance, anyone who tells you that money won't make you happy never had enough money to know whether it would or it wouldn't. This idea is born from those who try to make sense of why they don't have money. People justify it and try to make sense of their condition in life.

For example, my mother clipped coupons as though her life depended on it because that was her only play. She spent all of her time justifying those actions. I remember when she visited me in Beverly Hills long after I had made it financially. We went grocery shopping together and I told her, "Mom, grab six of the artichokes." She said in her southern accent, "OMG, son—I can buy those for one dollar less back home." I told her, "Mom, make it a dozen since I can't go broke one dollar at a time."

> *"Those brought up poor and middle class*
> *inherit the beliefs of the poor and the middle class."*

You see, my mom was still stuck with the beliefs of the poor and middle class long after it mattered. That is what people do—they defend what they have done to survive and then get stuck in this lower, poor condition.

Now, back to whether money will or will not make you happy. I can assure you money will not make you happy, nor will it make you unhappy. I have been happy and unhappy. I have been broke and I have been very rich. They have nothing to do with one another and whoever talks about them in the same conversation is someone justifying why they don't have money. One additional note on this, from personal experience: if you are going to be unhappy, be as rich as possible.

Financial freedom is two parts mental and one part mechanical. And you have to get your mental part right first. What I mean is that you probably need to lose your mind first, including many of the beliefs you were brought up with. For instance, getting rich is mostly a game of offense, not defense like my mother taught me. Taking risks today is the way to eliminate risk, but you have to take risks at the right time. Your daddy's advice was to always play defense with money. To get rich, you have to learn to be on offense most of the time, not defense.

Wealth knows no age or sex, and it doesn't care about your story—it shows no sympathy and has no feelings. It listens to no god. There is no age too young or too old: anyone can play the game, but you have to play the game of wealth on offense.

"If you are going to be unhappy, be as rich as possible."

To win at the game of money, you have to be on the field as an offensive player first. Later, once you are way ahead in the game of money, you can play defense. If you want to get rich, you can't stay on defense or be a spectator, and you need to have a strategy.

All that being said, it has never been easier to get rich than it is today and never more important. Just last year, 500,000 households in America became millionaires. Are you ready to get rich?

I am one of those people who figured out how to create wealth. I have become a millionaire hundreds of times over. I am telling you this to inspire you—you can do this. The wealth I have created was not because of my education; I totally wasted that. It wasn't because of my connections; I destroyed them all. And it wasn't because I was lucky; I have never been one of those. I also didn't take a company public or create some cool invention or some fancy app.

You hold in your hands information that will show you how to make and accumulate millions of dollars, even hundreds of millions of dollars. I would tell you this

15

booklet could make you a billionaire but I haven't done that yet, so I will only make claims to what I have done for myself and for others.

I only ask you to do three things:

1) Keep this booklet in your possession until you become a millionaire.

2) Share it with a friend. Here's the link: MillionaireBooklet.com

3) Once you get yours, help others do the same.

"Getting rich is mostly a game of offense, not defense."

Chapter 3

Step 1: The Millionaire Decision

As I said earlier, the biggest mistake is to think becoming a millionaire is impossible. People simply don't think it can happen. So the first thing you have to do is decide to become a millionaire, multimillionaire, or billionaire if you want. You have to decide and then you must reinforce that decision, over and over. Put a stake in the ground right now: "I am going to become very, very rich." I will not judge you negatively for making this decision. When you tell someone who has created wealth that you want to get rich, they will not frown or judge you negatively—they will pat you on the back and say something like, "Great, you can do it and, by the way, you should!"

"Put a stake in the ground right now: "I am going to become very, very rich."

Those who have created wealth understand that creating financial freedom is a worthy adventure. Is it possible for anyone? Remember, more than 80 percent of all millionaires today are self-made, what's called "first generational," meaning they created their millions without inheriting the money.

Now, before that little automatic voice in your head says for the millionth time, "I don't want to be rich," or, "I just want enough to be happy," you should understand two points: 1) Getting rich isn't just about you, and 2) Limiting yourself financially invalidates your abilities.

Most of us are convinced to settle for basic necessities: clothes, a house, transportation, time off, maybe an upper-management position, and some money in the bank. This is called the middle-class. The middle-class is for those who settle for just enough rather than striving for prosperity. The middle-class life is a compromise and it's selfish. When you compromise your finances, you become unable to help others because you are struggling to simply take care of yourself.

The other part of this is the constant invalidation of you! You are capable of way more than you know, so why set reasonable financial goals? For my entire life, I have had this constant gnawing in me that knows I can do more, achieve more, create more, give more, and help more. And I am most unhappy when I give up on that gnawing idea and most happy when I am pursuing it.

"Settling for a middle class life is a compromise and it's selfish."

But enough of the esoteric and back to the material world. You can earn $80,000 a year or $400,000 a year and still struggle, depending on where you live and your responsibility level. Just because someone makes more money than a person born in some starving village in a third-world country doesn't mean they are much better off. The argument is, "You have a cellphone, internet access, running water, and electricity—be grateful." That's code for, "make sense of your situation."

But not having enough money doesn't make sense. A man once told me, "How do you make sense of insanity? The answer is, you don't!" And not having enough money is insane. The idea that someone would only need enough to be "comfortable" or "adequately satisfied" or "have more than others" as a way to justify his or her condition is ridiculous. The middle class is billions of people convinced by politicians and media to turn your money over to those smarter than them, settle down in a nice house (reducing your ability to move for the next thirty years), and be a civil, law-abiding taxpayer who is grateful how much better off you have it than those who have less.

"Not having enough money is insane."

Make a decision right now to become a millionaire and debunk all the ideas that idolize the mythology of the middle class. The temporary comfort provided by the house, nice school, a couple of BMWs, a 401k, and two weeks off is nothing compared to creating massive wealth.

The first step to becoming a millionaire is to make a decision and that requires you lose your middle-class mind and then get your millionaire mindset. You must lose your small, defensive, take-no-risk thinking. It has never been easier to get rich, but it is still impossible if you don't change your mind. There is so much money in the world today and so many ways to create wealth, but it will not happen if you settle.

Many will disagree with me on this, but I believe millionaire is today's new middle class. In fact, many millionaires still find themselves struggling. If you want to get really rich, you will need 10X or 20X or even 100X of a million dollars.

"The first step to becoming super rich is decide and then you must lose your middle-class mind."

Use my 10X Planner and start affirming your multimillionaire status every morning, every night, and anytime you have a setback. Make the decision right now: "I am going to be very, very, very rich and I am going to help a lot of people in the process."

When you start to doubt the possibility, take out this little booklet and reread it and trust me to help you get there.

You don't need to trust yourself at this point—simply put your trust in someone who has done it. When I first started studying wealthy people, I put my trust in them because I could not yet trust myself.

Chapter 4

Step 2:
Millionaire Math

Your second step is to simply do the math. Did you know that most people will produce or be in contact with a million dollars in their lifetime? If you earn $50,000 a year for twenty years, you earn one million dollars.

For any goal to be achievable, you must believe in its possibility as a realistic and doable goal. The way to do this is simply by doing Million Dollar Math. How many different ways can you collect one million dollars? You should figure all of them out.

The purpose of this is to simplify the objective. In my bestselling webinar, "How to Become a Millionaire," I used the example of sticky notes. How would you collect a million sticky notes? First, you would ask if there are a million sticky notes on planet earth. Second, you would ask who has them, and third, you'd ask, "What do I need to do to collect them?" Do the math to create possibility, then create strategy.

Do the millionaire math and reinforce your millionaire possibility and your commitment to it. Wealth requires simple, basic math and any wealthy person will tell you this. After all getting to a million dollars is about numbers. But keep it simple. The best ideas are always simple.

"Do the math to create possibility, then create strategy."

I know couples I have worked with who, after doing the math, looked at each other and realized how irresponsible they had been. "We never did the math!," the husband told his wife. The wife said, "There are so many ways to get there." They could finally see what they had to do. Do the millionaire math. Keep it simple. The strategy will come after.

Here are a few ways to a million dollars:

Salary $50k x 20 years

Salary $100k x 10 years

Salary $250k x 4 years

Earn $114 per hour, every hour of the year

5,000 people buy a $200 product

2,000 people buy a $500 product

10,000 people buy a $100 product

1,000 people buy a $1000 product

5,000 people pay $17 per month for 12 months

2,000 people pay $42 per month for 12 months

1,000 people pay $83 per month for 12 months

500 people pay $167 per month for 12 months

300 people pay $278 per month for 12 months

Or do the bottom ten on this list and you'd earn 10 million in a year.

Chapter 5

Step 3:
Increase Income

Once you've done the math and realize how real it is to get super rich, you need focus on increasing your income streams. In the beginning, you simply set new income targets and then do whatever it takes to increase income, at first in increments, and then later in leaps.

At twenty-five, when I was struggling to make $3,000 a month, I quit bitching and acting like a baby about my income and committed to increasing it. The first target I set for myself was to simply make another $3,000 per month. I did the math and it was $750 a week or $100 per day or $10 more per hour—it became real to me.

I didn't change jobs, even though I didn't like my job. I used the job I had to learn how to grow my income. In the first month, I exceeded my target and made over $7,000 for the first time in my life, tracking for almost $84,000 a year if I could keep up that pace. I continued to focus on the simplicity of this and in the first twelve months I made almost $100,000. Not bad for twenty-six years old.

I was super excited and realized how important increments and surges in income are to validating confidence and possibility. When you quit bitching about money and start taking responsibility for increasing your income, it's amazing what happens and how quickly it can happen.

Money seems to flow to those who give it the most attention and who take the most responsibility for it.

Money never found me when I was complaining about it. Ever notice that the people who bitch about money are those who are the most broke?

> *"Money seems to flow to those who give it the most attention and take the most responsibility for it."*

If you are in a sales position, then you know what you need to do. Sell more! If you are not in sales, then look for every way possible to add income. Don't say you can't, it's a lie—anyone can create income. Go look for things you no longer want and put them up for sale. Don't even worry about how much or little you sell them for, sell them and prove to yourself you can increase your income. Whatever you can't sell, give away to charity and take a tax deduction. Instant tax credit is actually income in reverse, but I will save this calculation for a more in-depth book on wealth building. When you have nothing else to sell, go to your brother or sister's house and take away all the things they no longer want and sell it online to increase your income.

You could also get a second job waiting tables, giving massages, babysitting, pet sitting, teaching a language, driving for Uber, or panhandling.

A family once asked me to coach them on their business and, due to financial troubles they were having, I proposed they start selling some of their personal property. The husband said, "These ideas seem so beneath us!" I reminded him, "What's beneath you is living paycheck to paycheck and never having prosperity."

The broke groan, cry, belly-ache and moan while the rich take responsibility. If you want money, you must quit complaining, moping, crying, making excuses, and you have to drop the entitlement thing.

Whatever it takes, you are going to create prosperity.

Complaining, moaning, and groaning will not increase your income. Make the commitment to create wealth, be ethical on your journey, and do whatever it takes until you achieve it. Let's face it, being broke is unethical.

When you commit you will find a way and it never means you have to be unethical. Send my company referrals and I will pay you. For every company you refer to me for our online product, Cardone University, I will pay $500 when we close the deal. Get me one a week and I'll pay you $26,000 a year. Get me three a week and I will pay you $78,000 a year. Make $50,000 and I pay you another $78,000 in referral bonuses, I just cut the time it takes to get your first million dollars from twenty years to just under eight years. (Do the math. I saved you over 12 years.) Is that beneath you?

"The broke bitch and moan while the rich take responsibility."

There are so many ways to increase your income today. From internet sales at home writing blogs, editing for authors, releasing a podcast, creating affiliate programs, joining great network-marketing companies, and on and on. By the way, everyone should be involved in network marketing. Just the fact that you get access to an instant network of like-minded people committed to improving their conditions is wealth creation!

Now once you increase your income, then keep doing the math and keep increasing your income in increments until you can start increasing in surges. The surges will happen when you increase your skills and start making investments.

I remember the first time I made $100,000 in a year. I was blown away. I never imagined that one day I would make a hundred thousand in a month! These are surges and they expand your potential and confidence in your abilities. Then I remember the first time I made 100k in a month—my confidence soared!

I continued growing my skills, doing the math, increasing my income and then one day, sure enough, I made 100k in a day and then I did that in an hour!

I had to work up to this in increments until it was real to me. And no matter how much someone tries to tell you to simply think and grow rich, getting incremental income growth is vital to get your surges.

But for sure, no one ever gets rich without increasing income first. Either you increase the income through investors or through the sale of products and services—or both. The creation of wealth, especially early on, is not about saving or investing—it's about increasing your income flows.

For those who believe you must own or operate a business to get rich—it is not true. In fact, three out of four millionaires work for someone else. To increase flows, you must operate like you are a business. The reality is you are a business you don't start a business. And the value of your business, you, is based on your ability to produce income.

My daughters, are four and seven years of age. Both can produce income at will by exchanging their unique values with those who might be willing to exchange money with them. They don't need a business plan or a lemonade stand to increase income. They are a business in their own right. By the way, both of my children have more money put away than 50 percent of the US population.

"You are a business, you don't start a business."

Chapter 6

Step 4:
Who's Got My Money?

This is so simple, it's amazing and it's genius once you understand it. Simply ask yourself: "Who's got my money?" People get into business and make a business plan and never ask this simple question.

Make a list of who has your money, the money you want, and figure out what you can exchange with them. Whether you have a service, a product, or an idea, the question to ask yourself is always: "Who's got my money?" You don't need to make money, you need to connect with those who've already collected money, who have money, and exchange what you have (skills and knowledge) with what they have (money).

Start investing most of, if not all of, your time with those people on your list. Get your millionaire mentality wrapped around this idea and spend every waking hour and all your energy on serving those who need what you have.

At the age of twenty-nine, when I started my first company I spent all of my time getting in front of people who could buy my product and spent almost no time with those who couldn't and/or wouldn't.

My wife and I recently were at a conference and I reminded her, "Elena, there are only four to six people we need to meet here." When my staff travels with me to a convention I remind them, "Be nice to everyone but remember we are here to meet people who have our money." This must be your foremost focus. If you don't do this, you will miss opportunities and waste time with people who cannot and will not buy or invest in your ideas.

I sound like a bad, selfish and greedy man, don't I? Well, no one calls me a bad man when the bill comes for dinner and I pick it up. No one thinks I am selfish when they need a loan and I'm the only one that can help them because I am liquid. When you want to start a new business with me and I provide the funding, you will be glad I am focused on my finances.

This is just the hard, cold simple fact of building wealth—follow the money, as they say. If you spend all your time with people who can't pay you will end up being someone who can't pay. "Who's got my money," is one of the most powerful concepts in the creation of wealth and time.

> *"If you spend all your time with people who can't pay you will end being someone who can't pay."*

That being said the more people you can help, the more money you will have. If you want to make a billion dollars, simply help a billion people. The people who need the most help on this planet don't have much money. So they will need you to have money to invent the solutions to help them. Figure out a way to get help to a billion people, and you will likely end up with way more than a billion dollars. And you will end up with more than money, you'll end up with true wealth, friends, support, love, legacy and worldwide admiration.

But let's be clear, you aren't going to help a billion people without either having money or finding someone who does!

So ask yourself, "Who's got my money?" And keep asking until you have answers. Once you commit to this concept fully, the money will follow like magic. If you are one of those people who doesn't like to talk to people because you tell yourself you are an introvert or you're shy, get over it. Remind yourself you don't like just getting by or being broke either. When your goals are big enough, you will quit telling yourself lies and making lame excuses.

You're not going to become rich from your closet, garage or your living room. It doesn't happen. Every one of those garage billionaires got rich when they finally left the garage to sell their idea, invention or product.

"When your goals are big enough, you will quit telling yourself lies and making lame excuses."

On my way from being broke to banking my first $5 million, all I focused on was, "Who's got my money?" I was traveling 300 days a year for over six years knocking on the doors of prospective buyers (investors) of my business idea. I provided a service and they exchanged their money with me. I hated every moment of it. It was not something I wanted to do, liked to do, and I had to gut up everyday to do it. I did thousands of free meetings around the US and Canada, traveling at my own expense to make myself known, and find opportunities to get in front of qualified buyers in hopes I could raise money to sell my product and increase income.

Billionaire Mark Cuban was quoted saying, "The most important thing you must learn about any business is sales." Sales made simple is, "Who's got my money?"

Once you commit to asking this question, you will want to learn how to master sales and I can help you at CardoneUniversity.com. For now, make a list of who is qualified and make yourself known to them.

If you have a money shortage, it is because you are investing your time with the wrong people and you're not applying, "Who's got my money?" There is no shortage of money on this planet, so if you have none, it's about some deficiency you have regarding money. Time invested on, "Who's got my money?" will always, always, always result in money.

If you are getting in front of those who have money and coming away without it, you have to join me at CardoneUniversity.com and I will help you resolve those deficiencies.

But first, ask yourself, "Who's Got My Money?"

Chapter 7

Step 5:
Stay Broke

When you start increasing your income, stay broke. I said broke—not poor. I have a policy to never, ever have money sitting around. Once I start increasing income, I immediately moved the surpluses to sacred accounts that were out of my reach and marked for future investments.

As soon as I started increasing my income, I went to my employer and told him to withdraw 40 percent of my gross pay before taxes and direct deposit those funds into personal accounts I had set up. They said they couldn't do that. I said, "You do it for the IRS, you can do it for me." I set up three savings accounts, which I labeled something special, and treated these as sacred future investment accounts. (Never use 401k for these funds.)

I remember when I first heard Michael Douglas say in the movie Wall Street, "Money doesn't sleep." I thought to myself, "But it gets bored!"

I knew from watching other people handle money that when money sits around it gets spent, wasted, and blown. Because I didn't fully trust myself to have cash sitting around, as soon as I created these surplus monies I directed all of it to accounts reserved to make future investments and create future passive income flows.

At the time I was twenty-six years old when I started this, which allowed me to fund my first business, my second business, and my real estate company. But the real benefit of this strategy was it forced me to continue to produce and out-work my earlier results. There were months when I was making more money than I ever made and I would push the entire surplus into my sacred accounts. When I did this I couldn't pay my rent even though I was making more money than I'd ever made. I was forced to negotiate with my landlord for an extension of my rent. It was weird because everyone knew I was doing well, but I never had money. I was broke, not poor, and it worked.

This state of staying broke forced me to continue producing new revenue. I had seen so many people have financial success, then quit doing what created their success and then go backward financially. Staying broke forced me to keep reinforcing the actions that had already proven successful.

It seems human beings perform best out of necessity. Studying the super successful, and those who are not, I noticed huge differences. It is bizarre how the wealthy work like they are broke and those who need money the most don't. Still today I watch the pretenders sleep like they are rich while I am up like I am broke. We both deceive ourselves but with very different outcomes.

I spent thirty years deceiving myself like this and one day I woke up and realized I had more money than I could ever spend. Even today I go to sleep and wake up like I am broke and push for the next level, aware that things beyond my control could possibly, unlikely, put my finances at risk.

The same will happen to you. An idea plus hard work multiplied over long periods of time plus discipline will always equal success. There just comes a point in time when, well, you will be super rich and almost nothing can change that condition. But you have to put in the work. Ideas are great but they mean nothing without hard work over time plus discipline.

Idea + Hard Work x Time + Discipline = Success

At the age of twenty-five I had made real commitment to getting rich, I took my first idea and worked very hard every day to make it happen over long periods of time, exercising extreme discipline. This created success in the beginning, allowing me to have a little extra money. Then I duplicated this cycle using money. Saving money and adding work over long periods of time and using discipline with the money will create financial success. I invested the money in savings accounts while working my main business and spending none of the surplus money (discipline) on stuff. I then prepared to reinvest the surplus monies to create new businesses and new, in fact multiple, income flows.

From twenty-five to the age of fifty-one, there was no alcohol, parties, showing off, exotic cars, only one watch, and almost no vacations.

Without knowing what my second business might be or even what I would invest in, I continued to prepare myself for the day when I would expand. Stay broke, not poor, deprive yourself now for the possibility of financial freedom in the future. Or more poetically, pay the price today so you can pay any price tomorrow.

A guy recently asked me, "Why are you still working so hard?" I didn't want to go into a long philosophical explanation of how I am preparing for a major economic meltdown as I knew he was just being social, so I told him how much I loved my work in hopes to let it go at that. Then he started saying dumb stuff like, "You only live once you know." And then he topped it off with, "I never see you at the club anymore." I got bored with him, so I patted him on the shoulder and said, "You never see me at the club, and I never see you at the bank!"

"Pay the price today so you can pay any price tomorrow."

Chapter 8

Step 6:
Save to Invest, Don't Save to Save

Investing money is how you will get super rich. The only reason to save money is to one day invest money. I was brought up believing you should save money for emergencies, retirement, and that rainy day event. All those books I read about had wealthy people saving to make investments not to just simply save. Since the age of 26, I have been saving so one day I could invest and expand, not simply to have some disaster or emergency I could fund.

My first investment was when I was thirty-one years old. I had been saving for six years and operating like I was broke. A guy came to me after one of my seminars and had the idea to create a hands-on, in-house training company in which a team of people would go into a company and put new sales procedures in place to increase sales. I told him, "I will loan the new company $50,000, it has to be paid back in ninety days, I get a salary for my information and a percentage of profits, and I will never lend you another dime if you can't pay me back in ninety days—so make it work." At that time, I only had a couple hundred grand saved but my main income, my speaking career, had proved itself very dependable and was growing at the time.

I liked the idea because it was a symbiotic business, connected to my first one. Meaning I didn't have to take my attention off the first company to grow the second one and the first business would feed the second one. My new partner paid me back in ninety days and the new company paid me as much in the first year as my first business did. That's what I call surges or spikes, not just incremental income growth.

My third company was created a couple of years after the second business. I was thirty-five years old and had been studying real estate for almost five years. I had looked at hundreds of apartment buildings over that time and never had the courage to buy one. I finally pulled the trigger on my first deal. The deal was a forty-eight unit apartment building in Vista, California for $1.95 million and it required $350,000 for a down payment. That was a third of my total sacred accounts. I knew it was a good deal and I did it. It took me six years to find it and when I did I moved with speed on it. It cash-flowed in month one and every month after that. Ninety days later, I bought my second deal, thirty-eight units in Point Loma, California for $3 million. Three years later, I sold both properties and made over $5 million, while earning $100,000 a year in positive cash. That $850,000 investment netted me $5,300,000—a 600 percent return.

Eight years of staying broke, eight years of staying on offense to strengthen my first and second business, while safeguarding my sacred savings accounts set me up so that one day I could make a significant investment. That was the first time I made a million dollars at one time and in this case, it was 5 million in one swing. The truth is it took years of discipline, knowledge and courage to be in a position to seize the opportunity—not a lucky break. Most people aren't equipped to take advantage of moments because they don't have the money, they don't have the knowledge or the courage.

People don't create wealth because they never invest enough in a deal to get a big payoff. Significant wealth creators make big plays, not little ones.

To do this, you must have surpluses of cash and confidence. When you know it's the right thing, go all in fast. Speed is power. When you do, you are going to exhaust your sacred accounts you had been building. At those times, you must have complete confidence in the investment and in your previous income flows so that, if the investment takes longer to work or even fails, you still can rely on your earlier flows of income.

Sometimes I will go years without investing in a new business and simply focus on making my current businesses stronger. I don't gamble with money, I invest it and I want sure things. That means I need to know what I am doing and the investment should be a no-brainer. I literally go through every possible worst-case scenario calculation and if I can still make money, I go all in. When I do, I am willing to go broke and exhaust all my cash knowing I am not putting my family or those who depend on me at risk because the earlier income flows can support us.

"People never create wealth because they never invest enough in a deal to get a big payoff."

Last year, rather than buying more real estate, I invested in a jet, a Gulfstream 200. The real estate market at that time seemed overpriced to me and I couldn't make sense of buying more the way I calculate deals. I went broke again paying for the jet, forcing me to keep hustling. I justified the purchase believing it would get me in front of more customers and help me grow my existing businesses (income).

Almost anyone will tell you a jet is a terrible investment. Ask any accountant and they will all tell you it's a terrible investment. But none of them can buy a jet, either. Ask anyone who owns a jet and they will tell you, "Nothing about buying a jet makes financial sense until you understand the value of time."

I paid for the jet the first year I owned it because it allowed me to get in front of more qualified customers in shorter periods of time and I continue to repeat the formula of increasing income, saving to invest and grow in increments and surges preparing for future investments.

"Nothing about buying a jet makes financial sense until you understand the value of time."

35

Chapter 9

Step 7:
Multiple Flows of Income

Poor people try to replace flows of money while rich people are trying to supplement (add) flows. Creating multiple flows of income is the holy grail of creating financial freedom and true wealth. At twenty-five years of age, I was complaining about how little money I was making. Today, I have over fifty streams of income from five different companies excluding a handful of stocks and mutual funds which I despise.

Some of those flows are from the first business that I still own and operate. Some are little drips and some are like fire hoses. The flows all require different levels of attention. Some require tremendous energy, and others are much more passive flows. I appreciate and value them all and I never complain about any of them. Complaining about your money situation never seems to make you more money.

The most common mistake people make when creating multiple flows of income is walking away from the current one. The next most common mistake is moving to secondary flows that are not similar to the first and then being unable to give both proper attention.

When creating your second flow of income, make sure to closely connect something parallel or symbiotic to your current flow and never abandon the first flow. For instance, if you work at a company and earn a salary, keep improving on what you do for that company and look for ways to create a second flow parallel to what you are currently doing. Do it within the company you work for during the time you are at work.

"Complaining about your money situation never seems to make you more money."

Most people start a second flow outside of their work, get excited about it, start ignoring the first one, and then end up with one flow again. And then the second one they moved to is weaker than the first one ever was. When you add a second flow, make a commitment to never ignore the first one. If you join a network marketing company, use it to supplement your first flow (both ways) until at some time in the future you can step away from it and never miss it or have someone else manage it for you. Also, make the flows work both ways. Make your new network of people familiar with the first company where you are working and flow business back and forth, strengthening both flows and both companies.

Robert S. has a salaried job creating video content in my office. He was making $45,000 a year with my internet department. He listened to my advice and took on a second flow selling and earning commissions bringing that up to $90,000 a year. Then, he added a third flow by creating ad revenue for the GrantCardoneTV.com and produces another $45,000 a year for himself. I call this parallel or symbiotic flows because they work with what he is doing already. He didn't seek another job outside of work, he figured out how to create two more flows from the same position during the same period of time and uses his time off for self-improvement so he continues to be brighter, faster and more confident in his abilities so he can continue to expand.

Never turn your back on the primary flows until, if ever, the latter flows are so strong that nothing can possibly destroy or erode them. Even then, you should think long and hard before walking away from any income flow— no matter how small. The same thing holds true when growing your customer base. Never turn your back on customers who got you to where you are now. There comes a time when it does make sense to walk away, but it should be the exception—not the rule.

When I was selling cars I tapped out on how much I could sell, I looked for other things I could do within the dealership to increase my income and to help my customers and the dealer. I learned how to finance the car as well as sell them. Everyone won! The finance manager didn't want to stay late, the dealer didn't have to pay someone else a salary, the customer was taken care of by your boy GC, and I earned extra money— ultimately making myself more valuable to the company, the customers and myself.

"Never abandon the first flow."

Nothing creates financial confidence more than multiple strong flows of income. I have a billionaire friend who invested in my real estate portfolio. I remember when I sent him a check for $9,000. He called me and said, "GC, that was a nice little check you sent me today— good job." Nine thousand dollars and the guy is worth $3,400,000,000. Crazy, right?

To create multiple streams of income requires commitment and especially discipline in how you use your time and money. While this all seems oversimplified, simple works, and complex almost never works. This is a rule I have used for years by the way with building my business and my companies. Simple works.

First, increase your income, then add to your income by starting a second symbiotic flow, expanding on that thing you are already doing. Bank all additional money so that one day you can make investments. Know what you are investing in until it is not a gamble or a risk but a sure thing! This investment should create new flows and new wealth which will allow you to make new investments that will create additional, more passive, flows of income while never taking attention off the earlier ones.

And one day buy a jet so you can continue to go where you want when you want and continue the process and be the guy who gives the million dollars to charity!

Chapter 10

Step 8:
Repeat, Reinforce and Hyperfocus

You can, and should, be a millionaire. You can be a billionaire, deca-billionaire, or richer if you simply think bigger from the start and then hyperfocus, and repeat the steps I have laid out.

Regardless of what others suggest, getting rich doesn't just happen and it comes with lots of challenges. You will have to give up something, probably many things. The first thing you will have to give up is your middle-class mind. The next thing you will give up is what everyone else thinks is fun. For twenty-five years of my life, I paid the price. While others were traveling, taking holidays, playing golf, and going on adventures, I was either building financial success or preparing myself to do so.

The first sign you are on your way is when the people close to you start to question why you are working so hard. They'll say, "We never see you anymore," "What's happened to you?," "You never have time for us anymore," and on and on. When you start your wealth adventure, many will try to convince you it's not worth it. Some will tell you it is impossible. It is worth it. It is possible. And it is important!

Your wealth adventure will be complicated by a new awareness that you are short on skills. Early on, I realized how little I knew about how to connect with people, network, communicate, build rapport, and how little confidence I had. I didn't know how to sell, market, promote, build value, negotiate, close deals, or follow up customers. I couldn't handle disappointment and rejection and I wasn't even dealing with money yet.

For the first time in my life, I started investing in myself. I committed to learning and studying. Because I didn't like to read I even took courses on How to Study that were amazing and allowed me to learn anything—and like doing it!

One of your early steps is learning how to increase your income (step 3) and then who's got my money (step 4) and this is where most people fail. I was spending 10 hours a day minimum at work six days a week on these two simple things and the rest of the time on self-improvement and building the skills I was deficient in.

As I started having success using my new knowledge, I immediately experienced a renewed sense of confidence and belief in myself. For the first time in my life, I felt really, really good about myself. I started feeling confident with my abilities and became even more committed to success. Those around me became more critical of my new focus. This will happen to you and you need to be ready for it. You are the only one who has changed, so expect this because when you change you may be a threat to them. I remember when I started working on myself and a girl I was dating said, "Don't change, I love you just the way you are." I thought to myself, "This isn't about you, it's about me and what I want." My commitment to my self-improvement had become a threat to her unwillingness to self-improve.

"When you change you may become a threat to all those who don't."

If you truly are committed to becoming a millionaire, you will at some point need to change your environment, and by that I mean your friends and family. That doesn't mean you need to get rid of people—it just means you need to add new people. The old friends will just fall off as they will lose interest in you. You will be annoying to them. If you want to make it into the club of wealth, you must add new connections and that means you need to reach up, not sideways and not down. If you don't change your surroundings, you will not make it!

Make a list of people in your city that are super successful, on the move, who are interested in personal growth, active in charities, who invest time to improve the quality of their lives, and are not just complaining all the time. These are the people you should surround yourself with. I am one of those people. My wife, my kids, and the people who work at my companies are all committed to improving ourselves and helping others be the best they can be and achieve financial freedom.

People committed to success want other people to be successful. People committed to the status quo want to be surrounded by the status quo. If you don't have the kinds of people around you that you want, go get them. One way to find the right people is to continue investing in yourself. Go to conferences, meetings, join mastermind groups, and network marketing groups.

Don't spend time and money on things, toys, holidays, or moments, invest in the surest investment of your life – YOU. When it comes to your self-improvement and education, spend whatever you must. If you must borrow money to make yourself better—do it. Remember you are not just trying to pay the bills anymore, you are playing to become a millionaire, even super rich if you want. Find the technologies that can help you unleash the real potential in you.

When you implement these eight simple steps, I can promise you a few things:

1) It will be harder than you think.
2) It will be easier than you think.
3) You will achieve way more than you imagined possible.

In case you are wondering, can anyone get rich? I don't

know if anyone can, but I doubt just anyone will pick up this book and even fewer will keep it with them every day. I know you can make it if you simply do what is laid out here.

Remember to keep the Millionaire Booklet in your possession until you reach your first million away—and when you do, make me the first person you contact.

Your friend,
Grant Cardone

Your next step is to join me at Cardone University. Do it now.

CARDONE UNIVERSITY

- **Master the Art of Business and Commerce**
- **Fundamentals of Sales**
- **Become a Master Sales Person**
- **Understanding Buyer Personalities**
- **The Perfect Sales Process**
- **Getting Past the Gate Keeper**
- **Improving Customer Experience**
- **Branding and Marketing**
- **Social Media**
- **Theory of Closing the Sale**
- **Master the Art of the Close**
- **Cold Calling Made Simple**
- **Handling Incoming Calls**
- **Internet Conversion**
- **Prospecting & Networking**
- **100 Ways to Stay Motivated**
- **Personal Finance**
- **Follow Up Sold Business**
- **Follow Up Unsold Business**

Sign up today at
CARDONEUNIVERSITY.COM

Recommended Reads:

The 10X Rule by Grant Cardone

The Art of the Deal by Donald Trump

The Closers Survival Guide by Grant Cardone

The Intelligent Investor by Benjamin Graham

The Problems of Work by L. Ron Hubbard

The Richest Man in Babylon by George S. Classons

The Science of Getting Rich by Wallace D. Wattles

Sell or Be Sold by Grant Cardone

The Warren Buffet Way by Robert B. Hagstrom

Think and Grow Rich by Napoleon Hill